HEROIN

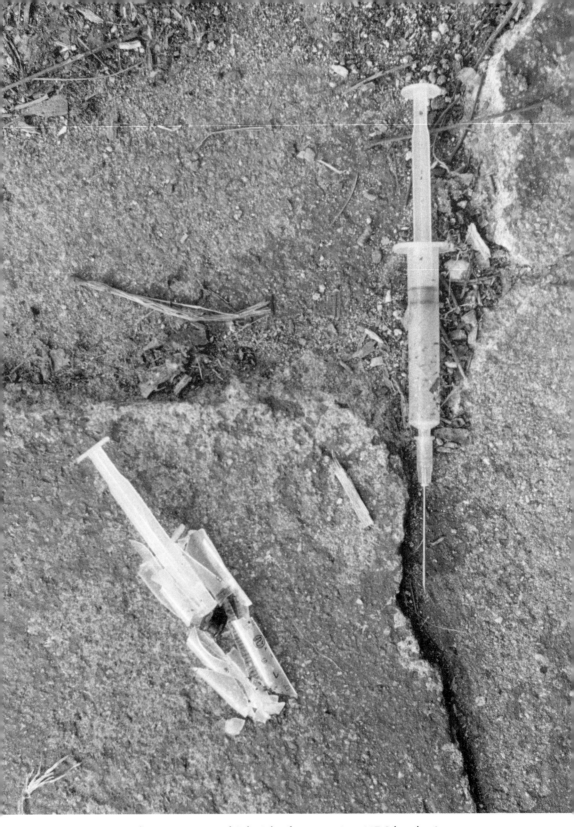

IV-drug users are at high risk of contracting AIDS by sharing needles.

HEROIN

Sandra Lee Smith

95-136

THE ROSEN PUBLISHING GROUP, INC.
NEW YORK

To my brother-in-law, Richard,
whose expertise in the prevention of substance abuse
has been invaluable not only to the writing of this book
but to our community.

The people pictured in this book are only models; they, in no way, practice or endorse the activities illustrated. Captions serve only to explain the subjects of photographs and do not in any way imply a connection between the real-life models and the staged situations shown.

Published in 1991, 1993 by The Rosen Publishing Group, Inc.
29 East 21st Street, New York, NY 10010

Revised Edition 1993

Copyright © 1991, 1993 by the Rosen Publishing Group, Inc.

Printed in Canada

Library of Congress Cataloging-in-Publication Data

Smith, Sandra Lee
    Heroin/by Sandra Lee Smith.
    (The Drug Abuse Prevention Library)
    Includes bibliographical references and index.
    Summary: Discusses heroin, its unique qualities and dangers, and counsels against illegal involvement with the drug.
        ISBN 0-8239-1685-5
        1. Heroin—Juvenile literature. 2. Heroin habit—Juvenile literature. [1. Heroin. 2. Drug Abuse.]
        I. Title II. Series
        HV5809.5S65 1991
        362.29'3—dc20   91-10676
                                           CIP
                                           AC

Contents

Introduction

*H*eroin, once known as the "heroic" drug, is one of the most addictive and destructive drugs available to teens today.

"I'm bored." Michael stretched out his long legs and shook back a lock of blond hair.

"Yeah," Jason agreed. "School sucks."

"Let's cut out of here."

"And go where?" Jason frowned, his dark brown skin crinkling around his eyes. "Ever since we quit smoking dope, life's been a drag."

Michael sighed. "What I wouldn't give for a joint right now!"

"I know. Where can we get one?"

Jason nodded toward a group of girls standing on the other side of the quad. "Maria has a stash in her locker."

"No kidding?" Michael straightened, paused for a minute, then sank back down. "We can't smoke now. If we get busted we'll be expelled for good."

Jason stood. "We can't get busted for asking."

"Cool it, Bro. I don't want to smoke, I just want to get high." Michael groaned as he watched his friend approach Maria. He half wanted him to come back; then again, if he scored...

Jason returned a few minutes later with Maria. Michael's interest perked up for the first time in days.

"I hear you wanna lift with no smoke." Maria smiled. "I've got just the thing."

Michael stood when he saw the foil in Maria's hand.

"A little Mexican tar, *hombre*."

Juan dropped the tray as the man brushed by. "Did you see him?" Juan barely noticed the tray Leo put back in his hand. "Wasn't that Shawn Clark?"

Leo cast Juan a wry glance. "You working with half a deck these days? Shawn Clark wouldn't be in a place like this." He

8 gestured at the crowded room where he and Juan volunteered every Saturday afternoon to help feed the homeless drug addicts who drifted in.

"It was him, I swear," Juan insisted as he began to clear the next row of tables.

"Come off it. Clark was our star quarterback. He's got to be playing for some big-time college team by now."

"I heard U.C.L.A. recruited him," Juan agreed. "Still..."

Just then the man they'd been staring at turned around. Juan and Leo both froze. It was Shawn Clark, but it wasn't the Shawn Clark they had known. The once muscular body was now washed-out skin over bare bones. His eyes were sunken in his lined and haggard face. His hair stood on end, unkempt and dirty.

"He looks like a hundred miles of bad road," Juan gasped.

"That's heroin for you," Leo murmured. "It wastes you."

The baby screamed.

Saralyn shuddered as she glanced at her son's red, puckered face. "Shut up!"

The baby continued to wail.

"I can't stand it." Saralyn stomped out of the room and slammed the door. Tears

The athlete works hard to develop his body. He chooses not to harm it with drugs.

10 rolled down her cheeks. If only she had some smack. It would calm her nerves.

Her fingers shook as she dialed the phone.

When Duane answered, she began to cry again.

"Saralyn, is that you?"

"Yes." She could barely speak.

"What's wrong?" Duane sounded worried. "You haven't taken anything, have you?"

"No," she managed to reply. "I need some stuff, D. I ache all over. My skin itches."

"Those are the symptoms of withdrawal. You'll get through."

"Can you bring me a candy bar or something?" She didn't want candy, she wanted the real thing. But she'd been craving sweets.

"Sure thing. Hang in there." Duane spoke firmly. "Remember your son. He needs to come off the drugs too."

Remorse coursed through Saralyn. Her son must feel as bad as she did. How was she to know he'd get high when she breast-fed him?

"It's okay, D. I'll make it." Saralyn hung up the phone and took a deep breath. Yes, she'd make it. She had to. She didn't want her son to go through the hell she had experienced.

Each of these people has been exposed to the ups and downs of heroin. The thing about heroin is that it always ends in a down.

Humans are miracles of creation. Each one of us is unique and designed to get as much or as little out of life as we want. Free will and self-determination allow us to gain our achievements in our own ways. It is impossible to accomplish anything, however, if we destroy ourselves. Heroin is a chemical that destroys the body and the mind.

Our bodies have enough strength and resilience to temporarily resist what is poisonous. But repeated exposure gradually breaks the system down. Eventually the system just stops working. When that happens, you die.

You are a valuable human being. There is no other being created quite like you, no other person can accomplish what you can. You need your body and mind to be able to work at full strength and capacity. You have your own purpose in life to fulfill, your own goals to achieve. It is your responsibility to see that you keep yourself in good working order.

Poppies are beautiful flowers, but they yield a deadly substance.

What Is Heroin?

*H*eroin is a chemical substance derived from the opium poppy. This beautiful flower grows in hot, dry climates. The pod left after the petals fall contains a white syrup that is collected by poppy growers. When the syrup dries, it hardens into a brown substance we call opium.

From opium, chemists extract many of our common drugs. Some of those drugs are used legally for medicinal purposes. Morphine and codeine are the most common ones. They are widely used by doctors as painkillers.

14   Heroin is also a common derivative, but it is illegal in most countries, including the United States. It is considered so harmful and dangerous that it is not even allowed to be used for medicinal purposes. Mainly that is because it is made from the garbage left over after making morphine.

That was not always the case. During the mid-nineteenth century a famous German chemist made heroin to help morphine addicts come off the drug. Morphine was widely used at the time as a painkiller.

The drug was considered a *heroic* substance. Soldiers from the Civil War up to World War I were given heroin to break them of their addiction to morphine. It was after the turn of the century that doctors began to realize that heroin addiction was far worse than morphine.

Now scientists have developed another chemical to assist the heroin addict. Methadone is used by some drug treatment centers throughout the United States to help heroin addicts withdraw. There is concern, however, that methadone is also addictive. In fact, some studies indicate that it is as addictive as heroin.

Manufacture of Heroin 15

It is illegal to grow opium poppies in the United States. Even if we could grow them, a laboratory is needed to process the syrup into the powders sold on the street. Such labs are also illegal.

Most of the international supply of opium comes from poppy farms in two major areas: the Golden Crescent and the Golden Triangle. Poppy farms and factories are illegal in those areas also. But the people are so poor that they risk punishment to grow the flowers.

The Golden Crescent is in the Middle East and includes the countries of Iran, Afghanistan, and Pakistan. The Golden Triangle is in South Asia and includes Laos, Burma, and Thailand. All of these countries are very poor. A farmer can earn 97 percent more money from a crop of poppies than from the same amount of grain.

Most of these countries are engaged in wars. Because of that, police action is focused on warfare, leaving little time and money to fight drug trafficking. Also, these countries need expensive weapons. Drugs are often exchanged for arms.

16   In the western United States heroin is imported from Mexico. *Mexican Brown* is a poorly processed grade of heroin made from poppies grown south of the border. It is of very low quality, but the demand for it is so high that the makers see no need to spend money to process a better quality.

These social and economic conditions make it difficult to control the production of opium poppies. As long as people will buy their product, these poor countries will produce opium.

Transporting opium to the United States is illegal. However, opium slips through customs in many ways. Because of the increased attention of law-enforcement agencies, the drug scene on the streets is changing. Shipments of marijuana, which is strong smelling and bulky, are decreasing while opium and cocaine importation is increasing. The more compact substances are easier to smuggle into the country.

Unfortunately, the demand for all these drugs is high. Dealing them on the black market and on the street involves millions of dollars. The power of that much money makes it very hard to control the various

Drug-sniffing dogs help law-enforcement officers to check luggage at airports.

18 sellers, dealers, and buyers. From the drug barons to the street dealers to the neighborhood pushers to the users themselves, greed and need rule supply and demand.

Because the market is illegal, it is not regulated. That leaves the business wide open to corruption, danger, and death. From the start of the chain in the Middle East and Southeast Asia, dirty laboratories begin the potential for death.

Buyers never know what purity or dosage they are getting in the packs of powder they buy. No laws control what is added to the substance. So a user faces not only addiction and the ill effects of the drug, but the possibility of overdose or poisoning or both.

Dealing the drugs is also dangerous. Heroin is illegal, so whatever level of the business you are involved in is criminal. Criminal activity not only is immoral but involves the dealer with immoral people. Those people are likely to cheat, steal, lie, and even kill. That happens at all levels, from the baron protecting his turf to the addicts who are so desperate for an injection that they kill for it.

You may think you are safe because friends or family supply your needs. But somewhere in your dealing you will come across a possibly life-threatening situation. It could be the quality of the heroin or the person you deal with.

Other Names for Heroin

The big H	Scag
H	Stuff
Smack	Elephant
Chi	Tiger
Dragon	Nanoo
No. 4	Gear
No. 3	China White
Harry	Black Tar
Junk	Chiva
Scat	Mexican Brown
Horse	Tar
Chinese	Mexican Tar

A heroin addict shoots up—injects heroin to get one of many fixes in a day.

CHAPTER 2

How Does Heroin Affect You?

*H*eroin is a narcotic. The word narcotic comes from the Greek word *narkosis,* which means benumbed. Physically, heroin numbs the senses.

Physical Effects

Our five senses enable us to survive in our environment. Taste, smell, touch, hearing, and sight feed messages to our brain so that we can react to what is around us. If we don't like what is around us, we have choices. We can change the environment, move to a new location, or ignore what is there. Most of us learn to function within the circumstances.

22 As teenagers it is not always possible to make changes. The choice to ignore is difficult, especially if the environment is depressing, lonely, or ugly. The addict's wish is to escape. Chemical substances deaden the senses and let one ignore the surroundings.

The problem with that form of escape is that whatever makes you want to escape doesn't change. Drugs wear off and there you are, still facing the same problems.

A first-time user of heroin often becomes violently ill, with vomiting and a severe headache. Peers or pushers say it will be better the second time. For some, it isn't. Occasional users often suffer from diarrhea, stomach and muscle cramps, and loss of appetite.

Heroin can be taken several ways. It can be smoked or swallowed, but neither way is very effective. The most common method of taking heroin is injecting it. *Skin-popping* is injecting the drug under the skin, not in a vein. A drug user's body builds up a resistance to almost anything it is given. Heroin is no exception. In order to get a high, a user needs more of it each time. Skin-popping soon becomes ineffective.

The user may then begin *mainlining,* | **23**
injecting heroin directly into a vein. With
frequent injections, veins may collapse.
When new veins are used, *tracks* may ap-
pear on a *junkie's* body. Sometimes a user
misses a vein. This can cause an abscess
or develop into blood poisoning.

There are several grades of heroin.
Many of them are poor. A user generally
filters the heroin into the needle through a
piece of cotton or a cigarette filter to get
rid of any clumps. This leaves some residue on the cotton or filter. This residue is
often diluted and given to a first-time user
with the mistaken idea that it won't be a
very strong dose. This procedure can be
dangerous, especially if unsterilized cotton
is used.

If you are allergic to heroin or any opi-
ate, you can become violently ill and even
die on the first fix. Heroin that has been
made and handled poorly, is not mea-
sured, or is mixed with poison can cause
overdose or death. There is no way of
knowing when or if that will happen.

An overdose can cause heart failure,
rapid heartbeat, shortness of breath, and
ringing in the ears or head. Some heroin
overdoses cause coma, or unconscious-

24 ness. That is extremely dangerous, as victims can fall and smother or drown in their own vomit.

Daily use of heroin causes extreme constipation and a loss of appetite. Many addicts suffer from malnutrition for one of two reasons: First, they are not hungry. Second, and more commonly, the constipation becomes so painful that they don't want to eat more food.

Emotional Effects

Most people get to heroin because they have been doing other drugs. As we have suggested, use of chemical substances is a form of escape. It is an emotional reaction to one's life situation. Instead of dealing with life, users choose to escape it.

Another emotional aspect of addiction to heroin and other substances is the *rip and run* thrill. Teenagers who do not see themselves as successful or do not see life as meaningful make a world for themselves that is filled with a series of daily purposes and successes.

The actual drug is not the purpose. It is the whole process of finding the stuff, getting the money for it, scoring the hit, and then riding the high. They are not

Counselors can help teens find a way out of the misery of drug addiction.

taking drugs, but *doing* drugs. Their day is a whole series of small, yet significant successes.

This false sense of purpose and accomplishment often replaces a teenager's view that life lacks real purpose and accomplishment.

Everyone can find some meaning and purpose in life. They can do so by searching deep within themselves and by setting and working toward goals. Choosing the escape of drugs leads only to a slow process of self- destruction. Repeated use of heroin or any chemical substance corrodes the brain, the organs, and the body. This path is a sure journey to death. Searching within and acting upon your values and goals is a road to life.

Running away from home makes many teenagers easy prey for drug pushers and pimps.

CHAPTER 3

How Do You Get Heroin?

*H*eroin is easy to get. In fact, most teens get it from friends. In the introduction, Michael and Jason were first introduced to smack by Maria and most likely continued to get it from her. You can, of course, get it on the streets.

Drug dealers try to work through a network of high school students for two reasons: it protects them from getting caught, and it makes it easier to move the drugs. They target popular figures such as sports heroes and leaders. Their purpose is to make *doing* drugs the "in" thing. It usually works.

The outside dealers are usually the gangs and pushers who get the heroin

28 from the border to the neighborhood. Because of the money involved, dealers and pushers do not operate within the law. They don't have to because their activities are already illegal. They lie, cheat, steal from one another, and sometimes murder.

These are the people who *handle* the heroin you buy. They are the ones who mix the concentrated heroin with other powders such as flour, sugar, chalk, baking soda, rat poison, and strychnine.

Keep in mind that they do not follow any standards. They are not under codes or rules. Therefore you have no way of knowing what the heroin has been mixed or *cut* with nor how strong it is. That is how overdoses occur.

The dealers and pushers are interested only in their own profit and protection. They have no concern for you, the consumer.

Friends

Friends who sell you drugs are like any other drug pusher. They don't care what they sell you. They often buy cheap heroin, poor quality mixed with powder, and sell that to you. They keep the good stuff for themselves.

When you buy heroin on the street you could be buying anything.

Many drug pushers in school sell to pay for their own habit. They "do" their profit. For example, they buy an eighth-of-an-ounce packet, or what they call an *eight ball*. They take some out for themselves and then *step on it*. That is a slang term meaning to add a powder to it to make it an eighth of an ounce again. Then they sell it as an eight ball. By the time you purchase a fix from a friend, it may be diluted or dangerously mixed with counteracting powders.

The pushers target popular students at school. Many of the students' friends don't

30 | even know that they do the big H. They
use their popularity to find a market for
their supply. They don't care what happens to the students who buy their goods
as long as they make enough profit to pay
for their own.

Pushers/Dealers

Most of you are probably saying to your-
selves, "I'd never get mixed up with a hard-
core pusher or a gang member." Most
students don't. They buy from friends,
and some even get their supply from family members. That is how drug dealers
operate. They develop a network of sup-
pliers within the school. They target
popular figures to create a false sense of
security. As we have pointed out, most of
those students sell to support their own
habit.

Drug dealers or pushers often offer free
hits to possible runners. They give free
smack until the targets are hooked. Then
when they have to start buying their own
stuff, the pusher tells them to sell some
and take their junk from the profits.

Some dealers offer free heroin to female
students until they are hooked. Then they
force the girls to prostitute themselves for

their supply. The dealers usually use the girls themselves at first. When they tire of the girls they start them on a career in the streets.

Through this process, the dealers insure that they have a market and a network in which to move the market. Most gang members do not use drugs themselves. They see the results and don't want to destroy themselves. All they want is profit. They have no concern for you personally. All you are to them is supply and demand.

Family

Unfortunately, many young people get drugs from family members. They often believe that they can trust such a supply. That is false security. The family member has to purchase the stuff from the same dealers the students at school do. It may not be the same person, but the heroin has traveled through the same unsavory chan-nels.

The fact that heroin is illegal in this country and is not even allowed for medi-cal purposes doubles its danger. Using even the cleanest heroin destroys your body, but unmeasured, unclean heroin can do so faster.

When parents drink and smoke, the stage is set for their teenagers to experiment with drugs.

CHAPTER 4

Why Do People Use Drugs?

*T*he largest population of substance abusers and addicts is the adult community. Therefore it should not surprise us to learn that most teenagers learn to do drugs from their parents.

All through childhood the cure for a problem is a pill. We see our parents have a drink to relax, to unwind, to party, and to escape. Many teenagers have seen their parents smoke marijuana or do cocaine or heroin or both.

Children copy their parents. That is the way it has been throughout the centuries. The drugs may not be the same, but the behavior of taking a substance to cure, forget, or tolerate a problem is.

34   If Mom and Dad have a couple of drinks to feel good at a party, why can't you do the same? Or even better, do a stronger drug? Smoking marijuana, snorting cocaine, hitting on smack, aren't you doing the same as they are when they have several drinks?

It is hard to tell the difference, except that alcohol is a legal drug. What needs to be looked at is why adults or teenagers need to do drugs at all. Often we need to help our parents break substance-abuse habits as much as we need to break them ourselves.

Curiosity

Some teens do drugs because they want to know what it feels like. Many try heroin for the same reason. If pot or coke is good, they think, the big H must be even better.

Along with curiosity is the element of risk: the dares from peers, the challenge of trying something new, the element of danger. That is a false sense of adventure.

The risk may not seem high when peers or family members have already done the big H. But each use has possible danger. There are better ways to satisfy your curiosity, be challenged, or face changes.

Resisting drugs could actually be a bigger challenge. The appeal of drugs is that escaping a problem through them is easier and requires less energy than fighting the problem. Many who say the big H is a challenge really are afraid to accept the true challenge of saying no.

35

Peer Pressure

If you are doing something that you know is wrong but you want to keep on doing it, you have an inner conflict. That usually results in guilt. To get rid of that feeling of guilt, it is normal to try to justify your actions.

Students who enjoy doing drugs often try to talk their friends into doing it because that makes their behavior seem acceptable. They can square it with themselves: "If everyone is doing the big H, it must be okay."

Peers who try to pressure you into taking heroin are not doing you a favor. They may be trying to get you to do it so that they can believe they are okay. As we have already seen, others may pressure you because they are trying to pay for their own habit.

Developing a strong sense of self-worth protects you from giving in to peer pressure.

36 Setting goals gives you a larger view to be able to make decisions that will be for your own good, not someone else's.

Stilling the Sense of Lack

Most teenage addicts say that their feelings of not being good enough are the major reason for doing drugs. Some feel that their families don't love them. If you think your parents are happiest when you're out of their hair, that causes a sense of being unwanted.

Unfortunately, parents get so caught up in the struggle to earn a living that it may seem they don't love you. Heroin will not fill that lack. It deadens the sense of loss but never substitutes for the real thing.

There are many ways to find people who will care about you. The best way to get people to love you and care about you is to love and care for someone else. Many other teenagers feel as lost as you do. Old people are lonely in your neighborhood. Little children, latchkey kids, are alone and in danger from the drug scene too.

You can decide to deaden your feeling of need or fill it. Helping other lost people fills that sense of being unloved or not needed. Your family may not have time for you, but someone does need you.

Living up to your responsibilities helps to create a positive self-image.

38   Other teenagers may have family love
but think their peers do not respect them.
Doing drugs does not buy respect. You
have seen that student pushers are under
pressure to build a market to sell their
drugs or to give belief to their lie that doing drugs is okay.

Other teenagers feel the way you do.
Find out who they are and together build
relationships that give you friends without
drugs.

After-school activities, school clubs,
community centers, and religious groups
have programs through which you can
help others in enjoyable projects.

Your life may be difficult. Your family
may not be what you want it to be. You
may not have the friends you think you
should have. No situations are ever per-
fect. Every person at one time or another
feels a sense of need. Every person at one
time or another feels that there is no purpose in life.

The difference among us is how we
react to those conditions. We always have
freedom to choose how to handle the situation. We can choose to run and hide. We
can choose to blame everyone else. We
can choose heroin or other drugs.

In an outpatient rehabilitation center, teenage heroin addicts receive daily doses of methadone as replacement therapy.

The point is that it *is* our choice. We can always choose to face our life as it is. We can change it. The only way to do that is with clear thinking.

There is no condition in this world that has not been faced by another human being. There is no condition that we cannot get out of. No one controls our will.

No matter how bad the circumstances seem, there is always somewhere to go, someone to help, and some way to climb out of it. Choosing drugs is one way. Choosing life is another.

Many teenagers lose friends to death from heroin overdose.

CHAPTER 5

The Trouble Heroin Will Cause

*H*eroin is not quite as swiftly dangerous as some people think. It numbs the brain and slowly corrodes the internal system. Yet many people do survive for years with daily use. Unfortunately, taking heroin regularly is addictive.

The definition of addiction is giving yourself over to something that becomes a habit. In other words, you enslave yourself to heroin. Instead of your controlling your own life, your life is controlled by the need for the big H. Taking heroin is selling yourself into slavery.

Health

Heroin is more damaging to mental health than to physical health. Addiction is psychological dependency. It leads to depression and often to suicide.

Think of the stories of humiliation and debilitation that slaves suffered in the past. Present-day heroin addicts are no different. They are often forced into prostitution, illegal drug-running, crime, and murder. That is partly because of the people they associate with. But it is also because doing heroin every day is very expensive. Most people addicted to heroin have trouble holding a job. They cannot concentrate on work, nor can they keep regular hours.

More dangerous than that, however, is the loss of self-worth one feels after committing crimes. Most heroin addicts need to deal with psychological problems as much as physical ones.

The dangers to the body include the risk of convulsive shock. Because of the way heroin is produced and marketed, there is a big risk of overdose or convulsions because of a bad mixture.

Have you ever seen someone in convulsions when overdosing? It is a frightening sight. The body may twitch so strongly that the person travels across the room jerking and gyrating. The person has no control of body functions and makes strange and ugly sounds.

Mucus pours out of the eyes and nose. The person drools or, worse, vomits. Lacking motor coordination, he or she may not spit the vomit out, causing himself to drown in it. He or she may urinate and defecate all over himself.

Prompt first aid may pull a person out of this condition. However, he or she may go into a coma for weeks, months, or years. Sometimes the experience damages part of the brain, disabling the person. Is the high from heroin worth that risk?

You might see friends or family smoke or inject heroin and, when nothing bad happens, think it is safe for you. You might be in a *shooting gallery* or place where people go for a fix and see your friends getting high with no problems. Keep in mind that all bodies react differently.

In reality, the biggest health danger from doing heroin are the indirect effects. More dangerous than the actual drug are the diseases you are exposed to. Most of

44 those diseases come from unsanitary injections. AIDS (acquired immune defi-
ciency syndrome), hepatitis B, and blood
poisoning (septicemia) are passed through
unsterile needles.

Junkies often *backwash*. They inject the
heroin, draw their own blood to rinse the
syringe, then reinject it to get every bit of
heroin and to make sure they've hit a vein.
Contact with blood is the main cause of
the passing on of diseases.

You may think that you would never
use an unsterile needle or *rig*. But many
teens find out too late that the needle may
have been washed, but washing is not ster-
ilizing. The fact is that sterile needles are
harder to get then heroin.

Other side effects are venereal diseases
from unprotected sex while on heroin, and
passing heroin on to a nursing infant
through breast milk. Continual use of
smack damages the reproductive organs
and causes infertility.

Heroin affects the mind and twists reality. That can cause people to overdose
accidentally. It can also cause such severe
depression that a person commits suicide.
Remember that heroin does not solve the
problem. It only hides it for a little while.

Family   **45**

Family relationships suffer when members
are on heroin. Users tend to withdraw
into themselves. Communication breaks
down, and relationships fall apart. Some
families practice "Tough Love" and kick

Loneliness and depression are frequent companions of drug
addicts.

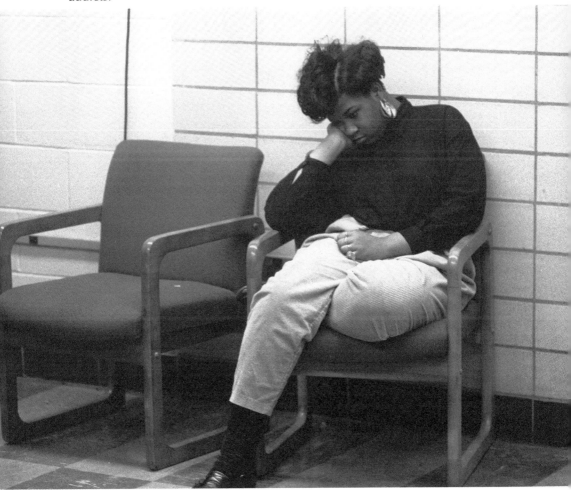

46 you out of the home until you are off drugs.

Most of these problems happen because of misunderstandings and fear. If you or any of your family show signs of withdrawing, it is important to seek family counseling. You need the emotional support of loved ones. They need to understand what you are going through.

Law

Heroin is an illegal narcotic. Possession or sale is a felony crime. Felony convictions result in hard time in prison.

First-time offenders caught using heroin for reasons not connected with other crimes such as selling, prostitution, or theft may be offered a diversion program. In such a program some states give teenagers the option of volunteering at their own expense to get: (1) counseling; (2) drug prevention education; and (3) periodic urinalysis. If they go through this program successfully, the charges can be dropped.

Not all states have this option. Nor do you have the choice if you are caught a second time. In such cases you are charged as a criminal.

People caught possessing heroin for **47** sale or selling the drug are charged with a higher class of felony. The penalties vary from state to state. In many states it is also a crime to have drug equipment such as syringes and pipes.

Another danger facing the user regarding the law is that once you are arrested, or *popped*, you may no longer be trusted by your *junkie* friends. They may think you are working with the police to turn them in. Some teenagers who have been arrested have a hard time scoring a hit.

An even more serious danger is that if someone is afraid you might snitch, he may give you a *hot shot*. That is an overdose of heroin or a dose laced with poison to kill you. This usually happens only if you burned someone on a deal.

Death

The final result of doing heroin is death. Everything you do, every decision you make, and every habit you repeat decides the quality of your life.

Life with heroin is not quality living. It is enslavement, disease, and decay. You are too valuable a human being to let heroin control your life.

Positive activities with positive people are a good defense
against the temptation to do drugs.

CHAPTER 6

How to Get Help

*I*t is important to remember that no situation is ever hopeless. Many people who take drugs may find that hard to believe. You may think your condition is worse than it really is. Don't forget that heroin changes your brain.

Addiction is difficult, but *withdrawal is possible*. Habits are hard to break, but *behavior can be changed*. Sickness is hard to overcome, but *people are healed*.

What to Do First

The first step toward help is admitting that you have a problem. The next step is to be willing to take action. The third step is to

49

50 find help. The final step is to commit yourself to the path to recovery.

The first two steps involve you. You make your own choices about your quality of life. It may seem that you are trapped in your life, but that is simply not so. You decide how you react to your situation. No one can control your thoughts or your wishes.

No one can force you to take drugs. No one can force you not to. Maybe incidents of control do occur. For example, if you are in a hospital or in jail you may not be able to shoot up on heroin. If you are enslaved or captured by a gang, you may be forced to take drugs. But look back on your actions. Your own choice of behavior put you in those situations.

If you have allowed circumstances to open you to addiction to heroin, you can still choose to get out. Once you face the need and decide to withdraw, there are many places to go for help.

Family, Friends, Religious Groups

The first place to go is to your family. Most drug addiction involves the whole family, either directly or indirectly. If other members of your family are involved in substance abuse, including alcohol, they will need help as much as you do.

Maybe they don't take part in substance abuse. But if they create problems for you through physical or psychological abuse or neglect or misunderstandings, group therapy can help you solve your differences. If your family relationship is healthy, you will need the love and support of family members to pull you through the ordeal.

Sometimes teenagers do not want their family to know they are involved in drugs. There are other choices. Other relatives or close friends can help you. School counselors can suggest help. Family doctors will treat you or refer you to someone who specializes in substance abuse. Many communities offer social services that include teen centers.

One of the best sources of help is a religious organization. Most of the people in such organizations are trained in counseling and have access to community services. For example, Phoenix, Arizona, has an organization called Clergy Against Drugs. These inner-city pastors are trained in assisting young people who want to withdraw from heroin or other substances. Most large cities have Jewish

52 Family Services, listed in the telephone book as a resource for those of the Jewish faith.

Rapha is a national organization that offers in-hospital or outpatient care for substance abusers (1-800-227-2547).

Teen Challenge has offices in big cities.

Heroin is a powerful addiction. Finding professional help is the next step.

Help Is a Phone Call Away

Whether your family is in on your decision or you are struggling alone, you will need trained assistance in withdrawing from heroin. Call a local hotline to find what is available in your area and which programs you can afford or qualify for.

Every major television network announces statewide hotline numbers to call for help. They usually follow a "Say No to Drugs" announcement.

The telephone book has listings in the Yellow Pages. Look in the "D" listings for *Drug Abuse Information and Treatment*. Call one of the clinics or centers and tell them what you need. If one is not the right place for you, they can refer you to other numbers.

If there are no drug listings in your area, try the "A" listings for *Alcoholism*.

You can get help without giving your name on an emergency hotline.

These centers work with the drug abuse centers.

The advantage of phoning for information is that you can be helped to some degree without giving any personal information. The volunteer can tell you which

53

54 clinics will treat you confidentially. Also, clinics range from free to over $2,000 per week in cost. Phoning can help you find the place you can afford. Always remember that help is just a phone call away.

Hotline Emergency

The inside cover of the phone book lists emergency hotlines. They usually have the words *drug, emotional, help,* or *hope* in the number. For example, the number in New York is 1-800-622 HELP for the National Institute on Drug Abuse Treatment Referral. In Arizona the number 1-800-475 HOPE is advertised on television. These are important to know if you are with an overdose victim. Call 911 or one of the emergency numbers.

Some states have emergency teams that specialize in overdoses. Arizona has an organization called TERROS. These men and women rush to the scene in plain clothes and treat the victim without involving the police. That can be an important consideration. The sight of uniforms or the sound of sirens can frighten an overdose victim into a heart attack.

Guidance

Every major metropolitan area and most counties have services for withdrawal from drugs. They range from government-funded projects to private hospitals. Religious organizations also provide counseling services.

Remember that substance abuse usually involves hidden causes. If you have been using heroin for any length of time, you will need to repair your thinking as well as heal your body. Good counseling and a relationship with a care group will help you to stay off the drug.

Kicking the habit will also mean changing some of your social habits. You might want to consider a new set of friends. Hanging around friends who are into drugs will be too great a temptation.

Treatment centers can introduce you to new friends who will understand what you are going through and can help you.

Treatment and Rehab Centers

Since withdrawal from heroin "cold turkey" can be painful, many are afraid to quit. That does not have to be the case.

56 Treatment centers offer controlled withdrawal with the help of other substances
such as methadone and maltrexone. Some
clinics employ acupuncture.

Such treatment enables a person to
come off the drug slowly. It also allows
him to function at work or school in a
normal routine. Withdrawal does not have
to be painful.

Unfortunately, many states do not offer
methadone to teenagers unless they have
failed one or two 21-day detoxification
programs.

The programs for teenagers that have
been most successful are the rehabilitation
centers where they live with other teens
coming off the drug.

Helping others is the best way to help
yourself. The advantage of living with
other addicts is that you can share experi-
ences. There is someone who understands
what you are going through.

Rehabilitation centers offer drug abusers a chance to take themselves away from
their old environment in a setting that is
drug-free. Through counseling and group
therapy, they learn ways to rebuild their
lives so that they can be free of depen-
dence on heroin or other drugs.

Alcoholic Anonymous and Narcotics Anonymous achieve their success rates by helping their members renew their relationship with family and God. If you belong to a religious organization, or even if you go to a new one where your past is not known, you will be strengthened.

So much of the battle with substance abuse is an inner struggle. Much of the appeal of any drug is emotional and mental. You want peace, freedom from stress, and a sense of well-being.

These can be found on a permanent basis, but not through drugs. Get in touch with your inner self, and strength will come to help you battle the temptation offered by drugs. Find a true and spiritual relationship, and you will find peace, security, well-being, and love.

57

Glossary

Explaining New Words

addiction Inability to resist the urge for a drug.

alternative Choice between two or more courses of action.

cold turkey Quitting the use of a drug without any help.

comatose State of being unconscious, caused by disease, injury, or poison.

constipation Difficult passage of hard, dry feces.

corrosive Gradually eating away, like rust.

cut To mix heroin with a powder.

derivative Made from another material.

eight ball Eighth of an ounce packet.

emulate To try to be like someone.

felony Serious crime that results in severe punishment.

hot shot Overdose of heroin, or a dose laced with poison designed to kill the user.

injection Placing of a substance directly
into the blood, usually with a needle.

junkie Person addicted to drugs.

laboratory Place where scientists work.

mainline To inject heroin directly into the
blood through a vein.

malnutrition Poor health caused by not
eating an adequate diet.

popped Arrested.

prosecute To charge in court with a
crime.

prostitute Person who is paid for per-
forming sexual acts.

rehabilitation Restoring to former
health, or putting back into good condition.

rig The needle and tourniquet used to
inject heroin.

rip and run Process of doing drugs in
which you *rip* or get the drug and then
run to find more.

scoring a hit Buying heroin.

shooting gallery Place where people
gather to get shots of heroin.

skin pop To inject heroin under the skin,
not directly into the vein.

step on it Slang term for taking some
heroin out of a packet and adding back
some kind of powder to make the
packet look full again.

Help List

- American Council for Drug Education
  204 Monroe Street
  Rockville, MD 20852
  (301) 294-0600

- National Clearinghouse for Alcohol and
    Drug Information
  P.O Box 2345
  Rockville, MD 20852
  (301) 468-2600

- Narcotics Anonymous
  World Service Office
  16155 Wyandotte Street
  Van Nuys, CA 91406

- National Federation of Parents for
    Drug-Free Youth
  8730 Georgia Avenue
  Silver Spring, MD 20910
  1-800-554-KIDS (5437)

- NIDA Clearinghouse for Drug
    Information
  P.O Box 416
  Kensington, MD 20795

For Further Reading

Ball, Jacqueline. *Everything You Need to Know about Drug Abuse*. New York: Rosen Publishing Group, Rev. ed., 1992.

Godfrey, Martin. *Heroin*. New York: Franklin Watts, 1987.

Jackson, Michael and Brude. *Doing Drugs*. New York: St. Martin's Press, 1983.

Kaplan, Leslie. *Coping with Peer Pressure*. New York: Rosen Publishing Group, 1990.

Kurland, Morton. *Coping with AIDS: Facts and Fears*. New York: Rosen Publishing Group, 1990.

Lee, Essie E. *Breaking the Connection*. New York: Julian Messner, 1988.

62 Morgan, H. Wayne. *Drugs in America*. New York: Syracuse University Press, 1981.

Smith, Sandra Lee. *Coping with Decision-Making*. New York: Rosen Publishing Group, 1989.

_____. *Coping through Self-Control*. New York: Rosen Publishing Group, 1991.

Sunshine, Linda; Wright, John. *The 100 Best Treatment Centers for Alcoholism and Drug Abuse*. New York: Avon Books, 1988.

Toma, David; Levey, Irv. *Toma Tells It Straight with Love*. New York: Bantam, Doubleday, Dell, 1981.

U.S. Department of Justice. *Drugs of Abuse*. Washington, D.C.: Drug Enforcement Agency, 1992.

Index

About the Author

Sandra Lee Smith has taught grades from kindergarten through college in California and Arizona.

In response to the President's Report, *A Nation at Risk*, Ms. Smith participated in a project involving Arizona State University, Phoenix Elementary School District, and an inner-city community in Phoenix. Participants in the project developed a holistic approach to education.

Photo Credits

Cover photo: Chuck Peterson
Photos on pages 2, 9, 25, 29, 32, 37, 40, 45, 48, 59: Chris Volpe; page 13: Gamma-Liaison/Dr. Allan W. King; page 17: Gamma-Liaison/Roger M. Richards; page 20: Chuck Peterson/Blackbirch Graphics; page 26: Gamma-Liaison/James Metropole; page 39: Wide World.

Design and Production: Blackbirch Graphics, Inc.